The Psalms of My Solitude

The Psalms of My Solitude

A Lifetime of Stillness

MICHELLE WOODWARD

TATE PUBLISHING
AND ENTERPRISES, LLC

Published by Tate Publishing & Enterprises, LLC
127 E. Trade Center Terrace | Mustang, Oklahoma 73064 USA
1.888.361.9473 | www.tatepublishing.com

Tate Publishing is committed to excellence in the publishing industry. The company reflects the philosophy established by the founders, based on Psalm 68:11,
"The Lord gave the word and great was the company of those who published it."

Book design copyright © 2013 by Tate Publishing, LLC. All rights reserved.
Cover design by Rodrigo Adolfo
Interior design by Jomel Pepito

Published in the United States of America

ISBN: 978-1-62295-263-2
Poetry / Subjects & Themes / Inspirational & Religious
13.02.08

Acknowledgments

First and foremost, I am thankful for the love God has given me directly and the love He has given me through the special relationships I now have. His love enables me to love others and to forgive and be forgiven.

To Jesus; for loving me so much that You gave Your life for me. Thank You for never forsaking me.

For my dearest darling, my best friend, my husband, Aaron; thank you for allowing the Lord to send you to me. Thank you for loving me, and thank you for allowing me to love you. Thank you for all the inspiration, support, and help you continue to give me. You have been such an encouragement to me. Each day is sweeter because we are together. I love you always, my LP.

For my daughters, Michelle and Elize; I now see why it is said that the Lord draws strength from children. You both are most precious and such an inspiration to me. Looking at you is like looking at the rarest and most beautiful flower made by God's own hands. God bless you and keep you both always.

For all my family and friends who have inspired, supported, and loved me completely.

No matter what we may face, the Lord our God, our Father, will never forsake His children for *pain is only temporary, but God's love is everlasting.*

For all those who hurt I pray that you will see through the pain with God's ultimate love, and that darkness shall not prevail in your heart. Amen.

Prologue

Numerous books have been written giving an account of people's lives, from how to be a successful entrepreneur to stories of men and women who have overcome great obstacles. This book will be different. Granted, while I will give some account of my own journey, I will also be frank and honest about truth. Some words I will pen will be difficult for me to reveal, however, I commit to this in order to shine a light on the secrets of our hearts…secrets that search to destroy ourselves among all others.

You will need to put aside all judgments and preconceived notions of all that is stored up in your mind, heart, soul, and spirit, unless it is spiritually based on God's great Word…truth.

I wanted this book to be a testimony of a new kind with the potential to be placed in the hands of young and old, rich and poor, saved and unsaved, famous and common. Originally, I wanted to cover topics like idolatry, fornication, pornography, drunkenness, abuse, adultery, murder of spirit and flesh, greed, and betrayal, etc., but one sin seemed to tie into the other, and with that, I would have had to write an encyclopedia series, and who has time for that? So, I spoke with the Holy Spirit about this, and He opened my eyes to what God had shown me all along…what every sin and imperfection has in common. Deception. *Deception is the seed by which all sin follows.* So this will be my central point.

It is time for us all to stop letting the world tell us what to believe and instead replace inconsistency with truth.

Lies are like drops of poison, plaguing this world with destruction and disease.

"Honesty is the best policy." Well, certainly it is but how many of us are truly honest? Do you lie to your spouse? Are you completely and entirely forthcoming with all information about yourself? Do you lie to your boss? Have you ever called in sick when you really weren't? Do you lie to your kids? Even telling them that Santa Claus or the Easter Bunny exists factually is a lie. Do you lie to yourself? I believe this is the most common untruth, including denial, exaggeration, fantasy, etc.

About four weeks ago, after enjoying dinner with my family, I asked everyone at the table to give each other a compliment, in an attempt to start demolishing some of the built-up tension and negativity between our children. When it was my husband's turn to compliment me, I expected him to say something casual and typical of what he would normally say. To my surprise he looked into my eyes and said, "I am thankful for how you always look out for us and help us all to do what is right." I was taken back so far that it felt like time had stopped for a moment, which proceeded with a river flowing from my eyes and a brick of emotion surfacing from my gut. In that moment, I realized that somewhere along the way I had buried many hurt feelings and frustrations and put a lid on them, which allowed me to ignore and deny myself, that I had been feeling unappreciated. I had been lying to myself instead of allowing God to deal with me.

I believe all of us lie to ourselves about few or many things for various reasons. Spouses lie to each other and themselves, opening the door for devices such as lust, fornication, also known as adultery. I myself had been in a relationship many years ago where my partner had been feeding lies about where he really was when he said he was playing basketball, at late-night meetings with his company, or just "going for a drive." Deep down I knew these were all lies, but I lied to myself in order to pretend that I believed him so that it wouldn't hurt as much. I never loved this person, but just the fact of someone being so callous and evil hurt deeply enough. Almost every word that came out of his mouth was a lie. After meeting some of the numerous "other women" and enduring physical and emotional abuse, I snapped one day and decided to take the matter into my own hands and repaid him for his cruelty, once again lying to myself that I needed to take charge instead of allowing God to deal with him and me. In the end, I got what I thought I had wanted but as it turned out, I hurt myself more than I hurt anyone. Most regretfully, it hurt my relationship with my Father.

How many of us believe our own thoughts as truth then proceed to build off of them? This includes businessmen, teachers, and even preachers. No one is exempt by a label, as we *all* will be held accountable.

Lies. They destroy everything in their path either immediately or over time. What are lies? Yes, they are untruth but what about something beyond? I believe lies are a refusal to give God control. It is the enemy deceiving us to hinder our relationship with God. No good *ever* comes of that. Anything and everything that is not in total agreement with God's and His Word is in fact a lie! Look around you.

After many years of being hurt and rejected even from a very young age, I finally gave up trying to be loved and gave it all to God. I was driving down Highway 281 one evening, weary of being so "alone" and rejected in this world, when I threw up my hands and said to God, "I give up, Lord. I can't do this anymore." Five days later, I met the love of my life… the one I had dreamed of years before and the one who's existence I had felt all my life. I always knew that I loved him, though I had not yet met him in the physical world. I had seen him in several dreams and visions throughout the years and saw the love we shared and would share.

I met him on a Tuesday night, August 1. I had finally stopped getting in the way and gave it all to God, and Viola, my best friend, was brought to me like an angel. Funny thing about that gift of free will. So many of us think that it is a ticket to feed our flesh, when it's actually a ticket for us to be happy and closer to God in peace. After meeting Aaron, I cried almost non-stop for three days, not because I was sad or depressed, but instead out of relief that we had finally found each other. It was utter happiness that my love and I were finally together. Aaron had later mentioned to me that he had prayed a very similar prayer to the one I prayed in my car that night, at right about the same time as I had. He too had always felt as if he was able to feel me out there somewhere. I remember us speaking on the phone for two weeks straight and then never leaving each other's side. To this day, we still enjoy spending all of our time together and are rarely ever apart. This is a blessing to us. We have since been through so much together, but we still can't stand to be apart as God's love transcends through us as we continue to grow stronger each day.

Let's take a look at some of the other ways that we lie to ourselves. One of the biggest problems I see this day-in-age is that most of us live in some form of deception, as if a wool blanket has been pulled over our eyes, that we may not clearly see truth. Remember, there is only one truth and the rest is what we have been deceived to believe. If I gave you a blue shirt and told you it was green, even if you believed me and allowed your mind to believe it was green, the shirt would still be blue. The truth would be that the shirt is blue, and the lie is that the shirt is green. You would then be deceived the moment you believe the shirt is green.

This is how most of the world is and you see it every day all around you. *We must guard our minds from the lies that creep in unannounced.*

When I was a child, my dad used to always tell me, "An idle mind is the devil's playground." Idle or not, if you don't guard your mind with the Word of God, Satan will enter every chance he gets. The human race has a tendency to allow its mind to be controlled and manipulated, sometimes to extremes. Curious fact about this is that the same people shouting, "No one is going to control me," are the same people who are deceived most. They are so deceived that they truly believe that they know best and sometimes all. So many of us are confused, but we only have ourselves to blame. We walk around this earth living in our own little bubble, in our own little world believing all is well when all the while we are floating around in a filthy bubble of lies blind to truth. One day that bubble will encounter an attack sharp enough to burst open the world of lies, and then your whole world will come crashing down. Who will be there to catch you? *Lies are like helium...they make you talk funny as they take you off into the clouds.*

Almost every night for three weeks, I had vision-like dreams mostly associated with large waves and water coming up from the bottom of the ocean to cover the land. In every one of these dreams, there were multitudes of people sitting and standing around simply watching and waiting to be taken under, as if they are unaware of their imminent demise. I shouted to them to get out of the way to safety, yet they seemed to be oblivious to the warnings. I believe this to be exactly how most of the world has become—*indifferent in deception.*

What is left that is ever weighed? "Time is up. Enough of the lies and carelessness! The Lord will soon return, and you will be left behind if you resist the alteration of your ways and commit yourself to Christ, right now. Free yourself and get out of bondage. Stop believing the lies of this world. Stop looking for self-gratification and ungodliness. You do not have time remaining. Ask for forgiveness so that you may come home. How can you argue with God? Why is there no urgency in your hearts? It is because of deception! All you have to do is repent now and give your life to Christ, our Father who gave His life for us."

Would you ever turn your back on your parents and deny they conceived you? Okay...what would you do if your children turned their backs on you, without reason or cause, when all you have done is give them life and love them? Sure, we are not perfect but imagine. How would you feel? Now magnify that feeling by eternity. How do you think it makes our heavenly Father feel when we turn our backs on Him? And He *is* perfect. He has never done us wrong or failed to help us, even though we deserve it not, regardless of what you may have been deceived to believe. Yes, He has feelings. He loves doesn't He? Think about it. All He wants is for us to allow Him to love us and accept

Him as our Father and us to love Him in return. Yet so many turn their backs to Him.

I think it is safe to say that those of us being deceived are *deceived unaware.* I don't know…maybe there are people that purposefully decide to believe lies instead of truth, both conscious and subconsciously, but for the rest of us, what are we to do? One thought that comes to mind is that we are brothers and sisters in Christ. It's our brothers and sisters out there who need our help.

If deception is the one seed in common with all sin and destruction, love must be the way back. Love will guide you home. It is my belief that at the root, every born human and even animal, desires to be loved. Regardless that some deny it, it is a fact. I believe this because we are created from God, and God is love. We are here because of His love. He created us out of His love. Your brothers and sisters want to be loved, your best friend wants to be loved, your mom and dad want to be loved, even your pets want to be loved. And God wants you to love Him most of all. So, if everyone wants to be loved, why is there so much hate in this world around us? I believe it is because of pain. Hope turned disappointment turned pain turned anger turned hate. Love is our security but the only perfect and true love that won't let us down is the love of our Father. Underneath it all, we thirst for His ultimate love.

Love is love. There is no "kind of love." Love is how God loves us, and we are to strive to that perfect love as much as humanly possible. Love is forever. When love exists, it cannot be stopped. Those of us who are starving for love and don't receive it are also those of us who turn to devices such as alcohol, pornography, food, promiscuity, or any form of addiction to fill the voids. *When love is missing, sin comes a hissing.* If those of us who turn to devices of these sorts would have been given love during pivotal moments in our lives, we would have far fewer hurting people such as prostitutes, strippers, murderers, pornographic media, and corrupted businessesmen. Yes, we are even deceived about love.

There was a long period in my life when I had numerous vivid and sometimes overpowering night visions of different spirits at work in the spiritual realm. Most of the time, when they realized that I was able to see them, they would attack me. One in particular would always taunt me, attempting to put fear in my heart. For years, I lacked the discernment to understand this evil that appeared in many different forms until one day when I received God's wisdom as He allowed me to understand. Since a young child, I battled rejection in the plural sense. On this particular night, I saw the battle in a more "human" aspect. In this vision, I awoke from slumber and standing before me to my right in the dim darkness was an empty figure. Empty in feeling yet with a heavy appearance. His face was as of darkness, and he wore an empty black cloak and hood. Across his chest, he wore a banner that read "Rejection." This was the same spirit that had been after me for so many years, but this night I clearly understood many of the battles I had faced before. After this night, any time he reappeared before me, I rebuked him in "Jesus's name," which gave me control in the authority of God. To put it plainly, rejection can really mess someone up, but as God showed me, it doesn't have to be that way, as He will never reject His children who seek Him. I pray that you will never be deceived into believing that you are alone. I pray that you will never be deceived into believing that you are not loved, for that will *never* be true!

There are countless forms of deception in this world, made more accessible as technology continues to advance. *If Satan the Deceiver can deceive someone into feeling rejected at some point in their life, he then has an open window to plant seeds and feed the weeds, which lead to sin and bondage.*

Deception. Some people allow themselves to be deceived because they believe the lie is easier to handle than the truth. But that's like crawling instead of running to get you where you want to go. It may be easier at that moment, but it will take a lot longer to get to where you are supposed to be! How fit are you? Don't allow yourself to be deceived into being deceived. It's just another vicious and destructive cycle.

Bottom line: To some degree, we all need to examine and reexamine our beliefs to realign our mind and spirit with God. Then forgive all and love your neighbor, for no one is above another. We are all guilty of sin and "fall short of the glory of God" (Romans 3:23). Even you. Jesus had to die for *all* our sins, not just the murderer or adulterer.

I pray that you will find my stories within poetry and selection of Psalms to be encouraging, comforting, and uplifting, to be a reminder that you are not alone. God our Father always has the answer to the troubles we face. He awaits with His arms wide open, to hold you and comfort you, His child, in His arms to make you whole again. Let Him love you!

Broken

She looked up into his face…
Silence and stillness became her refuge.
She couldn't understand his reasoning…
His justice.
At that single moment, she was left without
Security, comfort, protection,
Love.
He had ripped it from her fragile, little heart…
A single tear dripped from her hazel eyes.
Her curls fell low.

Seven years young, and today she turns eighteen.
On her own, she must learn to survive.
How tragic is the battle she will have
To fight for the rest of her life.

 LORD, how are they increased that trouble me!
Many are they that rise up against me.
Many there be which say of my soul,
There is no help for him in God. Se'-lah.
But thou, O LORD, art a shield for me;
My glory, and the lifter up of mine head.
I cried unto the LORD with my voice,
And he heard me out of his holy hill. Se'-lah.
I laid me down and slept;
I awakened; for the LORD sustained me.
I will not be afraid of ten thousands of people,
That have set themselves against me round about.
Arise, O LORD; save me, O my God:
For thou hast smitten all mine
enemies upon the cheekbone;
Thou hast broken the teeth of the ungodly.
Salvation belongeth unto the LORD:
Thy blessing is upon thy people. Se'-lah.

Psalm 3:1-8 (KJV)

The Flower That Flew

There once was a flower that was
Happiness and lived peacefully.
She was getting weak and got flewed away.
She met other flowers but they told She
That She was not flewing right,
She had to skit, skat, hit the road jack.
So She skitted, skatted and hitted the road jack.
But then She met Her and Her knewed
Something that She not did knew…
That was how to flew!
Her taught She and She flewed better
Than the other flowers.
The other flowers said,
"Help me, teach me how to flew,"
But She was smart so She said,
"Skit, skat, hit the road jack,"
And that was the end of that.

Break their teeth, O God, in their mouth:
Break out the great teeth of the young lions, O LORD.
Let them melt away as waters, which run continually:
When he bendeth his bow to shoot his arrows,
Let them be as cut in pieces.
As a snail, which melteth, let every one of them pass away:
Like the untimely birth of a woman,
That they may not see the sun.
Before your pots can feel the thorns,
He shall take them away as with a whirlwind,
Both living and in his wrath.
The righteous shall rejoice when he seeth the vengeance:
He shall wash his feet in the blood of the wicked.
So that a man shall say, Verily there
is a reward for the righteous:
Verily he is a God that judgeth in the earth.

Psalm 58:6-11 (KJV)

The Dog That Didn't Die

The dog was there where the tree was once planted.
The tree died so the dog found new life where
He could be by a tree like the one that died.
But that tree died too, so the dog lost all of his
Best friends and hated trees from then on.
The next day he met a boy and found
An even newer life.
But then the boy died and the dog was so sad
That he wept and found yet another life
That didn't die…that was happiness.
The dog lived happily ever after.
The end.

I will bless the LORD, who hath given me counsel:
My reins also instruct me in the night seasons.
I have set the LORD always before me:
Because he is at my right hand,
I shall not be moved.
Therefore my heart is glad, and my glory rejoiceth:
My flesh also shall rest in hope.
For thou wilt not leave my soul in hell;
Neither wilt thou suffer thine Holy One to see corruption.
Thou wilt shew me the path of life:
In thy presence is fullness of joy;
At thy right hand there are pleasures forever more.

Psalm 16:7-11 (KJV)

No Place

The darkness seems to come,
The deadliness seems to leave,
To haunt you in your dreams;
    Make sure you don't leave.

But when all the world has turned,
    You find there is no place.
Nowhere to hide, no refuge to find
From the sin, which seeks no grace.

The lonely spot within your life
Will no longer seem to leave
As your company has found you;
    No place.

Sing praises to the Lord, which dwelleth in Zi'-on:
Declare among the people his doings.
When he maketh inquisition for
blood, he remembereth them:
He forgotteth not the cry of the humble.
Have mercy upon me, O Lord;
Consider my trouble, which I suffer of them that hate me,
Thou that liftest me up from the gates of death:
That I may shew forth all thy praise in the
gates of the daughter of Zi'-on:
I will rejoice in thy salvation.
For the needy shall not always be forgotten:
The expectation of the poor shall not perish forever.
Arise, O Lord; let not men prevail:
Let the heathen be judged in thy sight.
Put them in fear, O Lord:
That the nations may know themselves
to be but men. Se'-lah.

Psalm 9:11-14, 18-20 (KJV)

Nothing

Ever been discouraged
Or feeling down and gray?
Have you ever tried to reach out
And find there's no one there?
Ever thought of turning to nothing
Just to find there is no way?

Ever lost your feelings in just one day?
Ever felt like going wrong instead of straight?

For feelings such as these leave you alone,
Full of fear.
It is then that the spirit of nothing
Taps on your window.
Will you let him in?

HOW long wilt thou forget me, O LORD? Forever?
How long wilt thou hide thy face from me?
How long shall I take counsel in my soul,
Having sorrow in my heart daily?
How long shall mine enemy be exalted over me?
Consider and hear me, O LORD my God:
Lighten mine eyes, lest I sleep the sleep of death;
Lest mine enemy say, I have prevailed against him;
And those that trouble me rejoice when I am moved.
But I have trusted in thy mercy;
My heart shall rejoice in thy salvation.
I will sing unto the LORD, because he
hath dealt bountifully with me.

Psalm 13:1-6 (KJV)

"the walls; do i rest ?"

The world is closing in on me. These words are fading.
Nothing is clear. My mind is warped with fear. Nothing
comes to good but everything comes to pass. i sit in my
cell and dream of outside fantastics. The caretaker yells
and yells and not lets me out. My time has been served.
i no longer should be in this place. Where is everything
going? Everything is passing me by; "don't leave me," i cry.
But no one stops to suffer with me. Am i the only soul
left to stay? i begin to think of death as it is. Where am i?
Everything is once again turning. "don't leave me!" I cry.
Yet still, no one stays to linger. i once had a bird, but it is
now dead. My feathers have flown away. Not even them
would stay. "what's happening?" I wonder. Everything
is so black. i cannot move so fast, for the keeper has
awakened. My only weapon i hold in my hand. Oh no, my
ink has run out. How will i now escape this darkness?

...

There is no light in this terrible place. The walls are now getting closer. Where did i go? Am i crippled? Once, my heart would beat, but now my pen has run out. The wind plays me a song. Will it take me away on its wings? They tell me to go home. But where is home? i don't even know where i lay. Where is this dreadful place where the keeper lets me die? I try to pray, but my pen has run out. All words are lost now. Where do i go? i see Fear, Darkness, and Pain. Is this home? Everything is once again moving so fast. i am unable to hold on to anything or anyone any longer. Everything is gone…my feathers! Even they have flown.

...

Do I stand? The light only comes now for a second. i cannot see my step clearly enough…i no longer exist. Is this where I stay? Or do i sink deeper into these clouds? Or am i drowning in water? i suffocate, but where am i? This place is gone. Every last piece of me has been destroyed by fast moving objects. Everyone has left me. Where have they gone? My keeper lets me not out to see. i can no longer hold on. Where am I?

The walls! do i rest?

Hear, O LORD, when I cry with my voice:
Have mercy also upon me, and answer me.
When thou saidst, Seek ye my face;
My heart said unto thee, Thy face, LORD, will I seek.
Hide not thy face far from me;
Put not thy servant away in anger:
Thou hast been my help;
Leave me not, neither forsake me, O God of my salvation.
When my father and my mother forsake me,
Then the LORD will take me up.

Psalm 27:7-10 (KJV)

My Vision Is Picasso

As he wrote with paint the beauty of a woman,
Distorted is the vision of my reflection.
Shatter the mirror and destroy the optical lens.
Deceitful is their image!

I have become numb.
My senses ail me.
I feel as a lifeless person
Looking upon the world.
All the while, I fall short to understand
What has happened to me and why.

I do not feel the pain of my teeth piercing my bottom lip.
I do not feel the joy music once brought my ears.
I do not taste the sweetness of delectable fruit.
I smell nothing around me.
I see in black and white…
My world has been robbed of its color.
I am an abstract being within this sensual hindrance.

*F*or thou hast possessed my reins:
Thou hast covered me in my mother's womb.
I will praise thee; for I am fearfully and wonderfully made:
Marvelous are thy works;
And that my soul knoweth right well.
How precious also are thy thoughts unto me,
O God! How great is the sum of them!
Search me, O God, and know my heart:
Try me, and know my thoughts:
And see if there be any wicked way in me,
And lead me in the way everlasting.

Psalm 139:13-14, 17, 23-24 (KJV)

Deception

The wind hallows a song
But the sea presents a name.
The earth trembles in fear
Still, I feel not the same.

Where do I walk on this jagged road of mine,
Whose acrid rocks lead through time?
Do I follow the easy road?
On the side…do I go?

The leaves are falling, telling me,
"There is hope, please just be."
But there are songs we must sing and
Names we must know.
The end of time is coming…
Which road must I go?

Show me thy ways, O Lord;
Teach me thy paths.
Lead me in thy truth, and teach me:
For thou art the God of my salvation;
On thee do I wait all the day.
The meek will he will guide in judgment:
And the meek will he teach his way.
The secret of the Lord is with them that fear him;
And he will show them his covenant.
Mine eyes are ever toward the Lord;
For he shall pluck my feet out of the net.
Let integrity and uprightness preserve me;
For I wait on thee.

Psalm 25:4-5, 9-10, 14-15, 21 (KJV)

//   //
_____

While I wonder to decease,
With some sort of strange disease,
All is without a heart unbroken
But the keeper, left unspoken.

If I feel my feelings out,
There will be a squall, no doubt.

"A prisoner to be kept,"
I imagined while I wept.
The one I seek over mountain peak
Is waiting still, or is it not?

My one left is bearing low
Like a field in a scarecrow.

Is there anything left to dream
After thoughts have been seen?

A shadow is flying through the river.
A fish is floating above the sea.
A pen is writing, asking why.
A prayer is spoken before one dies.

My sighs are nothing more than where I lie.
Revealing the dark while in the light.
Conspiracy.
Full of fright.

Make haste, O God, to deliver me;
Make haste to help me, O LORD!
Let them be ashamed and confounded
That seek after my soul:
Let them be turned backward,
And put to confusion, that desire my hurt.
Let them be turned back for a reward
of their shame that say,
Aha, aha.
Let all those that seek thee rejoice and be glad in thee:
And let such as love thy salvation say continually,
Let God be magnified!
But I am poor and needy:
Make haste unto thee, O God: thou
art my help and my deliverer;
O LORD, make no tarrying.

Psalm 70 (KJV)

A Two-Part Conversion of the Soul

At war with the mind,
Beating of the body,
Torment of the id.

Obscure? Certainly.
Silly are its claims.
Truth? Somewhere beneath the ruins,
Lost in the tumult of its garbage,
Like organized crime of the soul.

The battle was won.
The Victor am I!?

I am a perfect portrait.
I have the hidden layers.
Love is the black light.
The scene is the battlefield.
I am the Victor?!

True to myself, I hate not the opposing general.
The general? He was once my security,
My blood, who gave life to me.
It is he who placed the artillery in my hands
(In the wrong direction?)
To him, to Him!
I owe this anguish.

An evil disease, say they, cleaveth fast unto him:
And now that he lieth he shall rise up no more.
Yea, mine own familiar friend, in whom I trusted,
Which did eat of my bread, hath
lifted up his heel against me.
But thou, O Lord, be merciful unto me,
And raise me up, that I may requite them.
By this I know that thou favourest me,
Because mine enemy doth not triumph over me.
And as for me, thou upholdest me in my integrity,
And settest me before thy face forever.
Blessed be the Lord God of Is'-ra-el from everlasting,
And to everlasting.
A'-men, and A'-men.

Psalm 41:8-13 (KJV)

Lost

Lost in a world that has no name,
No place to love with nothing to gain.

Lost in a world to escape her light,
I'm lost but not terrified…in the end, I am right.

I run to resist the tempting call
Of those who are not lost at all.

I run to be who I am,
The one who others frequently damn.

I am lost in a world I wish not to change,
But only to escape his worldly rage.

I am lost, but I am not to be tempted…

I am lost, but I win.

The LORD is my shepherd;
I shall not want.
He maketh me to lie down in green pastures:
He leadeth me beside the still waters.
He restoreth my soul:
He leadeth in the paths of righteousness
for his name's sake.
Yea, though I walk through the valley
of the shadow of death,
I will fear no evil:
For thou art with me;
Thy rod and thy staff they comfort me.
Thou preparest a table before me in
the presence of mine enemies:
Thou annointest my head with oil;
My cup runneth over.
Surely goodness and mercy shall follow
me all the days of my life:
And I will dwell in the house of the LORD for ever.

Psalm 23 (KJV)

Stranger in My Doorway

Slumber interrupted,
Darkness surrounds me,
Alone in my consciousness.
Never to be free?

The sight in the distance,
Tall, shadowed but I see
He is the one who awoke me.
Never to be freed?

Too familiar is his face,
A stranger within him,
He is motionless with peril.
Hatred lies within.

As I sit up in bed
Anticipating in shadows,
Courage comes before me.
I must send him back to hallows.

His back is hunched
As an old fiend in pursuit,
His intent to frighten
And rob me from my youth.

He set out to provide me refuge
Before he was taken,
Used as a vessel,
My father, I was mistaken.

The pain he caused me
Led me to say
These words which follow
And freed me from this day.

"I told you, you are not
Welcome in my home!
Leave at once, I command you!"
Then he left me alone.

Why art thou cast down, O my soul?
And why art thou disquieted in me?
Hope thou in God:
For I shall yet praise him for the help of his countenance.
Yet the LORD will command his loving
kindness in the daytime,
And in the night his song shall be with me,
And my prayer unto the God of my life.

Psalm 42:5, 8 (KJV)

Self Beyond

The doubt within my heart,
As strong as it may seem,
Is only a taste of what may find
When opened thine eyes to thee.

The past has overcome
The depth that lies within
The promise, the trust,
The unforgiven of thee who lied and then…

The love that's felt deep within thy soul
Has undeniably come to doubt,
The mystery untold.

When yonder breaks, the truth revealed,
The love that overcometh will surely turn
To grey for those who find but not
The one who was loved for thyself,
Not for self beyond.

*J*udge me, O LORD;
For I have walked in mine integrity:
I have trusted also in the LORD;
Therefore I shall not slide.
Examine me, O LORD, and prove me;
Try my reins and my heart.
For thy loving kindness is before mine eyes:
And I have walked in thy truth.
I have not sat in vain persons,
Neither will I go in with dissemblers.
I have hated the congregation of evildoers;
And will not sit with the wicked.
I will wash mine hands in innocency:
So will I compass thine alter, O LORD:
That I may publish with the voice of thanksgiving,
And tell of all thy wondrous works.

Psalm 26:1-7 (KJV)

A Dying Soul

When trials of dark and loneliness spares
The life of one who really cares,
You mistakenly know the truth
That lies within the heart.
My soul has died for you to come.
The lonely spot…with me alone.
My fears are crying out to you with hope and faith,
Will you, the only one, do?
The question never fails to capture my mind
To take it not
To show me death, no life there ought.
When will I find the truth in you?
Is your love really true?
My time is standing still.
Without you, I am ill.
But what will it matter if you do not care?
I gave you my heart.
Will you leave it in despair?
Do not let all hope be gone.
My soul has died for you to come.
But if your love is really true,
You will understand what I feel for you.
My dying soul for you to come.

I sought the LORD, and he heard me,
And delivered me from all my fears.
They looked unto him, and were lightened:
And their faces were not ashamed.
This poor man cried, and the LORD heard him,
And saved him out of all his troubles.
The angel of the LORD encampeth
round about them that fear him,
And delivereth them.
The eyes of the LORD are upon the righteous,
And his ears are open unto their cry.
The face of the LORD is against them that do evil,
To cut off the remembrance of them from the earth.
The righteous cry, and the LORD heareth,
And delivereth them out of all their troubles.
The LORD is nigh unto them that are of a broken heart;
And saveth such as be of a contrite spirit.

Psalm 34:4-7, 15-18 (KJV)

A Verse from a Depth of My Soul

A familiar Stranger knocks upon my door.
He is accompanied by His Adversary.
I am brought memories reminiscent of a lonely spirit.
My Stranger reveals to me within
A vision, the possibility….

The image is encompassing.
The image of His eyes gazing down into mine with
His arms grasped tightly around me with
Love's promise to never let go.
He cherishes me, adores me, He becomes a
Part of my soul and it is in this place that
My inner continuation may reside free
And safe, existing throughout
All eternity.

But the company of this stranger releases to
Me the painful scent of an awakening.
All my existence,
I have but only longed for such truth,
Aware of its being,
Though never seeing it to know it…
I have yet to receive it.

Its absence leaves me forever in bondage.
It is an eternal flame upon brimstone
As my soul lingers above.
I have been chastised.

Upon the confrontation of the two Entities,
As I remain in the doorway faced
With the two Visitors,
An intruder approaches and enters wholly availed.
It is a painful memory of a past I have not met
In this life.
Of all that was which has ceased to be.
But the feelings remain...
'Tis how I know of its existence,
Though unseen to all who live.

I am left empty remembering what was,
What can be,
What may be,
What will not be.

I am a stranger to this world.

I accept...
I am true to my known self.

I will both lay me down in peace and sleep:
For thou LORD, only makest me dwell in safety.

Psalm 4:8 (KJV)

Nebula

If there were a time when nothing existed,
I was not there.
It is in the beauty of the Alpha
And the perfection of the Omega
Where my existence is defined.

In a time and place where such things
Have no bearing,
And looking into tomorrow would be
Looking into today,
This is where I reside.

How did I get there?
Where did "I" begin?
Such things are no mystery to that of I Am.

Beyond this, the reason for my
Eternity with no beginning…
You as you are.
A world, which is not a world.

In a vision of you,
An intimate portrait…
Your body…transparent.
Your heart…the galaxy.

In a world where words only serve
To confine and dilute your beauty and splendor,
And the perfection of your love,
The only justice to this magnificence is silence.

Gaze into my eyes,
Find that place which no one else can find
And there as our souls touch, we are one…
The vessel of perfect love…
The entity itself.

When I consider thy heavens,
The work of thy fingers,
The moon and the stars, which thou hast ordained;
What is man, that thou art mindful of him?
And the son of man, that thou visitest him?
For thou hast made him a little lower than the angels,
And hast crowned him with glory and honour.
Thou madest him to have dominion
over the works of thy hands;
Thou hast put all things under his feet:
O LORD, our Lord, how excellent is
thy name in all the earth!

Psalm 8:3-6, 9 (KJV)

Novel

Page 222…how I dream of you.
Page 333…you were down on one knee.
Page 1…no love seen, no answer done.
The end…you are more than a friend.

I will love thee, O LORD, my strength.
The LORD is my rock, and my fortress, and my deliverer;
My God, my strength, in whom I will trust;
My buckler, and the horn of my salvation,
And my high tower.
I will call upon the LORD, who is worthy to be praised:
So shall I be saved from mine enemies.

Psalm 18:1-3 (KJV)

Pain

Because of life
I need a way!

Because of you
I need a heart!

Because of love
I need a mind!

Because of life
I need a soul!

Because of the thought of living
Without you
I need pain!

*B*lessed is he that considereth the poor:
The LORD will deliver him in time of trouble.
The LORD will preserve him, and keep him alive;
And he shall be blessed upon the earth:
And thou wilt not deliver him unto
the will of his enemies.
The LORD will strengthen him upon
the bed of languishing:
Thou wilt make all his bed in his sickness.

Psalm 41:1-3 (KJV)

Caressed by Love

As his hand tenderly reaches to touch
The beautiful touch,
I hear the silent voices warmly speak out
The life of love.
I look into his hazel-green eyes and
I remember the supple,
Gentle evenings we spent together.

Remembering the first, as our lips
Watchfully caressed each other,
I felt a faint, smooth, subtle rush…the feeling of love.

The thought of my existence without him
Frightened me.

Our hands have met…it is here that I find my answer.
I now know, with him I shall spend eternity.
But without him, I shall no longer sacrifice
My love for him.

I resolve to show the pain in my soul.
I shall depart and dwell no more.
Love, it feels so beautiful.

Behold, how good and how pleasant it is
For brethren to dwell together in unity!
It is like the precious ointment upon the head,
That ran down upon the beard,
Even Aaron's beard:
That went down to the skirts of his garments;
As the dew of Hermon,
And as the dew that descended upon
the mountains of Zion:
For there the LORD commanded the
blessing, even life for evermore.

Psalm 133 (KJV)

Desire

Starlit green…Desire.
I'm lost in it.
My rivers reverse and the world is gone.
We are now in each other's space.
This scent drives me mad…I will not contain it.

Where am I?
I find myself in his mind, at his mercy.

Locked against his flesh, his finger moves to my forehead,
Feeling every second of my skin, edge of my eyes,
Cheeks and then chin.

I cannot bear it!
There, with his strength…he caresses my neck
As I inhale once more.
My eyes close in anticipation.
As our bodies decisively share warmth.
His strength is felt.

Set a watch, O LORD, before my mouth;
Keep the door of my lips.
Incline not my heart to any evil thing,
To practice wicked works with men that work iniquity:
And let me not eat of their dainties.

Psalm 141:3-4 (KJV)

Deliverance

Sounds of eternity…
As I lay surrounded in this field, filled
With the splendor of His creations,
I wonder if your existence is real.
I ponder to answer if what I feel inside
Is true to you.
I dream of your soul closely intertwined with
Mine, never releasing as your heart sours
Through my mind.
Whatever your true feelings are, let the wind carry
Us through these billows of time. Presently your
Yielding touch accompanies me as I give heed
To the sweet singing sparrows in the distance,
Whispering of their love for each other.

Their tender love rides the rhythm of their
Songs, over the hills and ever so gently
Delights my soul.

These sounds of eternity reveal what is truly ours.
Opening up our souls to the fields who
Are dying…but we are unique.
Never waiting to talk to our hearts,
The pain inside to redeem,
Set free, love the inner self, taking the
Place of the one who once loved.

I'm falling, not into the fields,
But into the deep, low,
Vital flame of your breath of life…
Behold, falling in love with you.

I call upon the LORD in distress:
The LORD answered me,
And set me in a large place.
The LORD is on my side:
I will not fear: what can man do unto me?

Psalm 118:5-6 (KJV)

Epiphany

I gazed up at the stars the night before
And as I became lost in their infinite splendor,
I realized the stars were not in our sky,
But rested endlessly in your eyes.

*T*he heavens declare the glory of God;
And the firmament sheweth his handywork.
Day unto day uttereth speech,
And night unto night sheweth knowledge.
There is no speech nor language,
Where their voice is not heard.
Their line is gone out through all the earth,
And their words to the end of the world.
In them hath he set a tabernacle for the sun,
Which is as a bridegroom coming out of his chamber,
And rejoiceth as a strong man to run a race.
His going forth is from the end of the heaven,
And his circuit unto the ends of it:
And there is nothing hid from the heat thereof.

Psalm 19:1-6 (KJV)

Veracity

Nothing ever left me in despair so much
As the moment when I lovingly laced my fingers in his,
Held him tightly,
And he didn't hold back.

*U*nto thee will I cry,
O LORD, my rock;
Be not silent to me:
Lest, if thou be silent to me,
I become like them that go down into the pit.
Hear the voice of my supplications,
When I cry unto thee,
When I lift up my hands toward thy holy oracle.
Blessed be the LORD,
Because he hath hear the voice of my supplications.
The LORD is my strength is my strength and my shield;
My heart trusted in him,
And I am helped:
Therefore my heart greatly rejoiceth;
And with my song will I praise him.
The LORD is their strength,
And he is the saving strength of his anointed.

Psalm 28:1-2, 6-8 (KJV)

Mi Graine

A shade of yellow is screaming in my ear.
Blinding is the color of energy.
Nonsense spinning all around me,
Orbiting my brain…
Make it stop!
I am cold. My bones quiver with illness.
I am a prisoner of this world, within this universe.
I may not flee to give in to combat
The alien in my bodice.
I am forced to endure it and remain awake.
My stomach is as a volcano unscheduled to erupt,
Hot and dishonest to remain contained.
My friend, my vision, begins to fail me…
All incitement angers the intruder within.

*D*epart from me, all ye workers of iniquity;
For the Lord hath heard the voice of my weeping.
The Lord hath heard my supplication;
The Lord will receive my prayer.
Let all mine enemies be ashamed and sore vexed:
Let them return and be ashamed suddenly.

Psalm 6:8-10 (KJV)

Stationary Spirit

I dare not desire crow's feet or a dagger in my heart.
Who is born to be broken and torn apart?
My refuge has fled…
Is now agony in my head.

Blood red stained kaleidoscopes
Have become my spectacles.

Yearning to wash away the crimson,
And trying with no avail,
I will shatter my own existence
To become clean without fail.

"No! You may not have a hand in my
Destiny, for I am the author,
And you are a chapter badly spent!"

So lift from me your forked tongue
To pierce the filthy armor surrounding your soul.
I am free, unbound by you.
You are a glacier in my ocean that will be your end.
Steer away, head another course,
Or your fate will be ill within!

In thee, O LORD, do I put my trust:
Let me never be put to confusion.
Deliver me in thy righteousness,
And cause me to escape:
Incline thine ear unto me,
And save me.

Psalm 71:1-2 (KJV)

Director; Stage 7; Take 1

Here in this translucent structure, I am suddenly
Made aware of the rising storm gathering above.
I am led outside as my gaze is set upon the
Horned cloud in our brilliantly blue sky.
Drizzles touch the ground and tickle my
Eyes, yet do not obstruct my view.
Pressing forward, this creature in our sky
Becomes visibly violent, bouncing in his moves,
Devouring all other clouds in his path.

I question why this is no wind tunnel…it is a being.
Once again my eyes are taken as I move forward
And once more view the merit of our sky. Bright
Clouds have parted and between them,
A crystal ocean
Smooth as silk and clear as sparkling
Radiance dazzles in splendor.
He speaks to me in all His glory as I am compelled
To reach out and ever so gently embrace
This ocean in our heavens…

I have now reached the structure across
My path and with both hands,
I urgently unfasten the doors…a multitude of familiar
People obliviously stand behind them. Imperatively I warn
Them all to, "Leave, leave at once!" before they are abruptly
Imprisoned by the birthing storm, but still they remain
With no urgency in their hearts.
I have told them of the ocean in the sky but I
Cannot force their will…and so, I must depart.
The vision He has blessed me with is the
Voice of truth that He is near.

*O*pen to me the gates of righteousness:
I will go into them,
And I will praise the LORD:
This gate of the LORD,
Into which the righteous shall enter.
I will praise thee: for thou hast heard me,
And art become my salvation.

Psalm 118:19-21 (KJV)

Elements

Despair, grief, torment, rage.
These are the devils of my age.
Rising above the enchantment of your hands,
I am strong, I am wise,
I am greater than man.

The fool hath said in his heart, There is no God.
They are corrupt, they have done abominable works,
There is none that doeth good.
The LORD looked down from heaven
upon the children of men,
To see if there were any that did understand,
And seek God.
They are all gone aside,
They are all together become filthy:
There is none that doeth good,
No, not one.

Psalm 14:1-3 (KJV)

My Solitude

Here we are once again…
Looking into your eyes, listening to your words.
Oh, how I love you ceaselessly.
And then you become the person I despise.
That person with the intent of wounding me
At every turn with your words, your hands.
I begin to sink into the lonely abyss I
Have come to know so well.
I am no longer able to see the endless colors
Of your eyes as they transform to grey.
My ears become numb and I no longer interpret
The words which drip from your tongue.

You seem to hate me with the utmost intensity.
I do not understand what has become
Of you in that solitary moment
When your love for me soured.
I no longer recognize what lies behind your eyes.
You are strange to me.
It stops! The asinine runs dry…you glare at me vacantly,
I realize you are awaiting an answer.
But how can you expect me to answer
When you sent me away?
It is not just to abandon me hastily and presume me
To await your return.

You lie to yourself.
You lie to me.
You declare me responsible for your treason.
I am guilty only of loving you.
I warrant no ill deeds,
Yet you deliver me into the hands of an enemy.
My only weakness is my love for you and
It has left me broken and dry.
What solitude have I left?

*H*elp, LORD; for the godly man ceaseth;
For the faithful fail from among the children of men.
They speak vanity every one with his neighbor:
With flattering lips and with a double heart do they speak.
The LORD shall cut off all flattering lips,
And the tongue that speaketh proud things:
Who have said, With our tongue will we prevail;
Our lips are our own: who is lord over us?
For the oppression of the poor,
For the sighing of the needy,
Now will I arise, saith the LORD;
I will set him in safety from him that puffeth at him.
The words of the LORD are pure words:
As silver tried in a furnace of earth,
Purified seven times.
Thou shalt keep them, O LORD,
Thou shalt preserve them from this generation forever.
The wicked walk on every side,
When the vilest men are exalted.

Psalm 12 (KJV)

Noxious Whispers

Lying silently still...
Three moons pass and suns set.
Lights bright, lights dim
But still we remain faithfully at each other's sides.
While the frantic world passes us by,
He has found a door left open in which to
Decimate with his every intention.
Time stands still for this short moment...
The earth freezes.
Still we remain by each other's sides,
Unaware of our potential demise.
Enter in does he...wholly availed.
The door in which he uses is painted with deceit,
The name above it reads "Fear."

You were unaware.
He took you, smothered you, rocked you to sleep
As a baby nestled in his mother's bosom,
Unconscious to her ill intent.
Who is this that you have trusted to enter our abode?

No longer is there a need for question.
I see him in your eyes.
He stole your face…made it his.
Tainted life pours from his tongue.
A burning fire rages beneath his eyes.
His strength is horrid,
His voice, a devil.

Lies are spoken to me as he attempts
To open my door,
Like a burglar lurking as an innocent guest.
I let him in not.
My punishment is color upon my skin
And cancer beneath.
Lash after lash I know his father...
It is not my Father.
Resentment, jealously, strife, vengeance
And wrath are his vehicle.
But I ride with him not.

My armor is strong and my strength is his equal.
I should allow this hurt to ail me?
Or shall I fight with what my Father has given me?

I find my strength as we wrestle in
Combat for the saving of the soul,
For the stealing of the soul.
"In the name of the Father, you will not hurt me!"

His eyes glare crimson into mine as his
Tongue scowls to me in laughter.
"Ha! You are stupid!"
His claws persist to force my head back
With my hair as his bridle as
He remains mounted upon me.
I speak to the one I love, "You are taken."
But my love does not respond.

My words are intercepted by this malevolence…
"Good…maybe you should kill me."
My answer to this absurdity?
"I would never kill you."
He then threatens me.
"You would never, for I would haunt you."

What world am I in that time stands still?
I must defeat this to save my love!
To save me from his grief!

"Who are you," I command, "What are you?"
"Who is who?" is his only reply.

I am left with one command…
"Leave him alone!"

The clocked ticked once more.
My tear finally fell to the floor.

The one I love fell one to me
With all his strength diminished.
He remembered nothing.

...

As I write this, I hear his whispers.

...

Why standest thou afar off, O LORD?
Why hidest thyself in time of trouble?
The wicked in his pride doth persecute the poor:
Let them be taken in the devices that they have imagined.
His ways are always grievous;
Thy judgments are far above out of his sight:
As for all his enemies, he puffeth at them.
He hath said in his heart, I shall not be moved:
For I shall never be in adversity.
His mouth is full of cursing and deceit and fraud:
Under his tongue is mischief and vanity.
Arise, O LORD; O God, lift thine
hand: forget not the humble.
Wherefore doth the wicked contemn God?
He hath said in his heart, thou will not require it.
Thou hast seen it;
For thou beholdest mischief and spite,
To requite it with thy hand:

The poor committeth himself unto thee;
Thou art the helper of the fatherless.
The LORD is King forever and ever:
The heathen are perished out of his land.

LORD, thou hast heard the desire of the humble:
Thou wilt prepare their heart,
Thou wilt cause thine ear to hear:
To judge the fatherless and the oppressed,
That the man of the earth may no more oppress.

Psalm 10:1-2, 5-7, 12-14, 16-18 (KJV)

Security

A voice once told me
I was never to believe.
But a vision then came to me and
I saw everything there was to see.
I heard a little whisper
So faint, and silent yet true…
It declared, "Without faith, love, and
Kindness, I do not have you."
So I told that little voice that came to me and said,
"There's always something out there,
But there is nothing ever to dread."

*F*or he shall give his angels charge over thee,
To keep thee in all thy ways.
They shall bear thee up in their hands,
Lest thou dash thy foot against a stone.
Thou shalt tread upon the lion and adder:
The young lion and the dragon shalt
thou trample under feet.
Because he hath set his love upon me,
Therefore I will deliver him:
I will set him on high,
Because he hath known my name.
He shall call upon me, and I will answer him:
I will be with him in trouble;
I will deliver him, and honour him.
With long life I will satisfy him,
And show him my salvation.

Psalm 91:11-16 (KJV)

The Sea Within Me

I tried to fly where no one went.
I tried and failed, but I try again.
This flight is unknown to those within this sea.
The sea is in control with no pardon to me.
I've flown before above this land afar.
But I have not flown until I am gone.
The day I leave, once more, again,
I will fly until I forget.

In the LORD put I my trust:
How say ye to my soul, Flee as a bird to your mountain?
For, lo, the wicked bend their bow,
They make ready their arrow upon the string,
That they may privily shoot at the upright in heart.
If the foundations be destroyed,
What can the righteous do?

Psalm 11:1-3 (KJV)

Hour upon Hour

Your answers are truth to me.
Your guidance is my refuge.
Hour upon hour darkness attempts to hinder me,
But You are my lamplight guiding me to safe harbor.

Though I live blinded by darkness,
You have given me sight more clearly
Than my eyes can see.
And it is with my eyes taken and un-relied upon
That I walk the straight line with You by my side,
My hand in Yours.

When I became weakened from the
Continuous murder of my spirit,
You never left me.
You comforted me and wiped away my tears.
You taught me to be strong and wise.

Everyone failed me, everyone pained me.
But my eyes remained shut
So that I may see You.
The flesh is my enemy...
I long to be home with You.

The LORD is the portion of mine
inheritance and of my cup:
Thou maintainest my lot.
The lines are fallen unto me in pleasant places;
Yea, I have a goodly heritage.
Thou wilt shew my the path of life:
In thy presence is fullness of joy:
At thy right hand there are pleasures for evermore.

Psalm 16:5-6, 11 (KJV)

The Last Chapter

Awaking with the sun, a final journey has begun.
Journey's past to leave, onward forward I perceive.

The veil of past shall cover me…I see no
More…only what is meant to be.
Journey in this present vessel leading
To calamity unknown to me.

On this road, I stared beneath,
Out from this chaos, our eyes locked suddenly.

His demise was apparent…all present discerned.
He was a thief in disguise; nothing from this earth.

He was commanded to stop me from my journey,
And from all that made it hurting.

The earth stopped. I was a moment in time.
He left this world with my curses;
No longer were they mine.

The sun shared its warmth;
It shined its light upon my heart
Revealing the showers of blessings
From which I shall never depart.

A healing through pain, a final journey began.
An end to this nature; the pain of man.

O give thanks unto the Lord; for he is good:
because his mercy endureth for ever.
Let Israel now say, that his mercy endureth for ever.
Let the house of Aaron now say, that
his mercy endureth for ever.
Let them now that fear the Lord say,
that his mercy endureth for ever.

I called upon the Lord in distress: the Lord
answered me, and set me in a large place.
The Lord is on my side; I will not fear:
what can man do unto me?

Psalm 118: 1-6 (KJV)

The Psalm of My Supplication

The Lord sayeth unto me,
"Behold my child, the waters
Cometh from the deep."

In the midst of my sorrow,
From the torrent of my waters,
A light shined upon me, for I have seen his face.
Glory be to the Father.

Silence fell upon my ears.
Tongues of silence encompassed me.

A bodice of pain, I was within…
My Father standing before me
As His child let him in.
He wore a robe of pure glory.
A rod of power and majesty stood beside Him.
Resting above, a crown of excellence and nobility.
He is the King Who Lives.

Beaming with eternal light, His lips spoke unto me,
His words flowing through my imprisoned pain.

Humbly standing before Him,
My eyes fell on my inferior limb.
Outstretched to Him, I see the wrist
Marked with scars.
The origin of my scars, I did not know.

His words again fell on me.
The result of which something stirred,
Frantically attempting to escape His truth.

Alas, my Savior took hold…
From the marking upon my wrist He
Unleashed three serpents from within.
Their lengths were massive, all of
Opposing colors and girths.

He took hold of them until it was done.
As the last thief left me, full of rabid anger,
The serpent lashed at my spirit.
And they were no more.

Plea for Deliverance
(A Non-canonical Psalm)

1. Surely a maggot cannot praise thee nor a grave worm recount thy loving-kindness.

2. But the living can praise thee, even those who stumble can laud thee. In revealing

3. thy kindness to them and by thy righteousness thou dost enlighten them. For in thy hand is the soul of every

4. living thing; the breath of all flesh hast thou given. Deal with us, O Lord,

5. according to thy goodness, according to thy great mercy, and according to thy many righteous deeds. The Lord

6. has heeded the voice of those who love his name and has not deprived them of his loving kindness.

7. Blessed be the Lord, who executes righteous deeds, crowning his saints

8. with loving-kindness and mercy. My soul cries out to praise thy name, to sing high praises

9. for thy loving deeds, to proclaim thy faithfulness—
of praise of thee there is no end. Near death

10. was I for my sins, and my iniquities have sold me to
the grave; but thou didst save me,

11. O Lord, according to thy great mercy, and according
to thy many righteous deeds. Indeed have I

12. loved thy name, and in thy protection have I found
refuge. When I remember thy might my heart

13. is brave, and upon thy mercies do I lean. Forgive my
sin, O Lord,

14. and purify me from my iniquity. Vouchsafe me a
spirit of faith and knowledge, and let me not be
dishonored

15. in ruin. Let not Satan rule over me, nor an unclean
spirit; neither let pain nor the evil

16. inclination take possession of my bones. For thou, O
Lord, art my praise, and in thee do I hope

17. all the day. Let my brothers rejoice with me and
the house of my father, who are astonished by
the graciousness...

18. For e[ver] I will rejoice in thee.

Reference:
Psalm scroll translation
Plea for Deliverance
(A Non-canonical Psalm)
Sanders, J. A. The Psalms Scroll of Qumran
Cave 11 (11QPsa). Discoveries in the
Judaean Desert, IV. Oxford, 1965.